BLOODY History of America

AMERICA'S BLOODY HISTORY
FROM
COLUMBUS
TO THE
GOLD RUSH

BLOODY History of America

AMERICA'S BLOODY HISTORY
FROM
COLUMBUS
TO THE
GOLD RUSH

KIERON CONNOLLY

Enslow Publishing
101 W. 23rd Street
Suite 240
New York, NY 10011
USA
enslow.com

This edition published in 2018 by:

Enslow Publishing, LLC
101 W. 23rd Street, Suite 240
New York, NY 10011

Additional end matter copyright
© 2018 by Enslow Publishing, LLC.

© 2018 Amber Books, Ltd.

Library of Congress Cataloging-in-Publication Data
Names: Connolly, Kieron, author.
Title: America's bloody history from Columbus to the Gold Rush / Kieron
  Connolly.
Description: New York, NY : Enslow Publishing, 2018. | Series: Bloody history
  of America | Includes index. | Audience: Grades 7–12.
Identifiers: LCCN 2017031474 | ISBN 9780766091771 (library bound)
  | ISBN 9780766095540 (paperback)
Subjects: LCSH: United States—History—Juvenile literature.
Classification: LCC E178.3 .C754 2017 | DDC 973—dc23
LC record available at https://lccn.loc.gov/2017031474

Printed in China

To Our Readers: We have done our best to make sure all websites in this book were active and appropriate when we went to press. However, the author and the publisher have no control over and assume no liability for the material available on those websites or on any websites they may link to. Any comments or suggestions can be sent by email to customerservice@enslow.com.

Photo Credits: Cover, pp. 3, 6 Everett Historical/Shutterstock.com; Alamy: pp. 15 (World History Archive), 17 (Jason O. Watson/historical-markers inc), 18 (The Protected Art Archive), 32 (Chronicle), 38 (Niday Picture Library), 39 (Stocktrek Images), 59 (Universal Images Group), 72 (Glasshouse Images), 73 (Andy Murphy); Alamy/Everett Collection: pp. 12, 34, 68; Alamy/Granger Collection: pp. 11, 13, 19, 36, 52, 61, 64; Alamy/North Wind Picture Archive: pp. 20, 21, 22, 23, 26, 29, 30, 54, 60, 62, 65, 77, 79; Art-Tech: p. 35; Getty Images: p. 58 (Universal Images Group); Getty Images/Archive Photos: pp. 27, 75; Getty Images/Bettmann: p. 67; Library of Congress: pp. 8, 9, 25, 43-50 all, 56, 57, 70, 74, 76.

CONTENTS

Though Christopher Columbus was not the first European to land on American soil, his journey in 1492 led to widespread, permanent settlement in North and South America by Europeans.

INTRODUCTION

TODAY THE UNITED STATES IS THE SIZE OF A CONTINENT AND STILL the most powerful country in the world. Yet 250 years ago it didn't even exist. The Declaration of Independence in 1776 may have proclaimed the ideals of "life, liberty and the pursuit of happiness," but America's rise has been colored by wars, rebellions and racial conflict.

That the United States rose to dominance partly through wars and conflict may not be a surprise. But when you reflect on American history—bloody or otherwise—you might not automatically picture US troops occupying Mexico City in 1847, or the British, long defeated in the Revolutionary War, coming back in 1814 to set Washington on fire.

This book traces the story of the United States from Columbus and the first contact between Europeans and Native Americans in the late fifteenth century to America's Gold Rush and the western migration that followed. It is the story of the gradual expansion of the country from the original 13 states to reach across the continent, of the ill treatment of Native Americans, of slavery, and of the conflict with Great Britain that led to the American Revolution. It is the narrative of religious hysteria as expressed in the Salem witch trials in the seventeenth century, and it is about how the values of the Founding Fathers laid down in the Bill of Rights—such as freedom of speech, the free exercise of religion, and the division between states' rights and those of the federal government—have continued to shape America.

CHAPTER 1

A NEW WORLD

BETWEEN 1492 AND THE 1760S, AMERICA WAS TRANSFORMED FROM a formerly isolated continent to one that, for free Europeans, represented liberty and opportunity. For its native peoples, convicts, and African slaves, however, it meant disease, displacement, and servitude. The New World would have a bloody birth.

It is now most commonly accepted that the First Americans were people from Northeast Asia who lived between 12,000 and 10,000 BCE, and who walked from Asia into America. Whereas today 55 miles (89 km) of water separates Siberia and Alaska, during the last great Ice Age the sea level may have been about 300 ft (90 m) lower, allowing a grassy patch of land to develop between the two continents. If the first Americans didn't cross on foot, it is suggested that they migrated by boat, and then

Popularly known as the discoverer of America, Christopher Columbus died in 1506—still maintaining that the Americas were not a separate continent but part of Asia.

COLUMBUS TAKING POSSESSION OF THE NEW COUNTRY.

Christopher Columbus was attempting to find a western route to Asia when in 1492 he happened upon the Bahamas. His subsequent voyages explored the Caribbean and parts of Central and South America but never North America.

edged their way down the Pacific coast before moving east and south across the continent. Whatever way they came, that is where they came from.

There were later migrations, too. The ancestors of the Inuit probably crossed the Bering Strait in boats about 5,000 years ago, and, in around 1000 CE, Leif Erikson established a Norse settlement that we now know as Vinland on the tip of Newfoundland. His, however, would be a less successful migration. Within a century Vinland had been abandoned.

Estimates vary wildly, but it is now believed that there were between five and 12 million Native Americans north of Mexico by the end of the fifteenth century. They were not a single society, but numerous tribes that, while connected through trading networks, spoke different languages and were often hostile to each other.

There were also whole societies that had risen and fallen by 1300 CE, long before the Europeans appeared. The sophisticated people who built the Cahokia mounds in Illinois or the settlement in Pueblo Pintado, New Mexico—works quite unlike anything constructed by the surviving tribes—still puzzle archaeologists today.

Then, in 1492, the North American continent changed forever when Genoese explorer Christopher Columbus crossed the Atlantic Ocean seeking a new sea route to the Far East and stumbled across the Caribbean. The first waves of exploration, conquest, and colonization by the Spanish, French, and English that followed may have been led by greed, guns, or God, but in all cases the newcomers brought the same weapon, and one they didn't realize they possessed: germs.

DISEASE

Isolated from the rest of the world, the peoples of the Americas had never been exposed to the common cold, influenza, leprosy, typhoid, the bubonic plague, measles, cholera, and, most importantly, the smallpox virus. While many people in Europe still died of smallpox, Europeans had, over centuries of exposure, built up some immunity to the virus. The Native Americans had no such immunity.

While the Spanish first carried their diseases into Florida and Mississippi, in the north, the French presence in the St. Lawrence Valley eradicated most of the Huron Native Americans and Iroquois during the seventeenth century. The English played their part, too, the settlement of Plymouth being built by the Mayflower pilgrims on the site of an Native American village that English-born viruses had wiped out.

Even as late as the 1760s, smallpox remained a major killer among Native Americans. Using it as a form of germ warfare during the Pontiac Rebellion, British commander Jeffrey Amherst gave Native American chiefs infected blankets from a smallpox hospital, urging his men "to try every other method that can serve to extirpate this execrable race."

Did the Europeans catch any diseases in return? It has been argued that they carried back from America the syphilis bacterium, but the debate on whether this was the origin of syphilis in the Old World is still ongoing.

Certainly most of the deadliest infections went one way; by 1650, it is estimated that the Native American population was reduced to

AS LATE AS THE 1760S, SMALLPOX REMAINED A MAJOR KILLER AMONG NATIVE AMERICANS.

one-tenth its number before European contact. For North America, this could have meant a reduction from five million people down to just 500,000.

In tackling diseases contracted from Europeans, Native Americans in Florida tended their sick by (*left*) cutting into the skull to remove diseased blood and (*right*) fumigating to remove toxins.

POTATOES, HORSES, AND COWS

The transfer of plant and animal life between the Americas and the rest of the world after 1492 was not just mutually beneficial; it was revolutionary. Not only did it change what people ate, but also how much they ate, how they farmed, and how many people they could feed. That meant it changed how societies developed.

The Spanish and English explorers brought home potatoes, tomatoes, avocados, chillies, turkeys, and tobacco. In America, the changes were even greater. Horses had died out there around 10,000 BCE but were reintroduced by the Europeans, who also brought rice, sugar cane, alcohol, pigs, sheep, donkeys, cattle, and wheat—which allowed the previously unpromising soil of American prairies to become agricultural land.

Smoking tobacco quickly proved popular when introduced to Europe, although in 1604 King James I of England warned that it was "dangerous to the lungs."

NAMING THE NEW WORLD

Christopher Columbus, although celebrated across the US, never actually set foot on what is today the United States. His four voyages were to the Caribbean islands and Central and South America, and he always maintained that the Americas were part of Asia.

Although the continent is named after Florentine traveler Amerigo Vespucci, he didn't discover America either, being no more than a lowly member of expeditions to the New World after Columbus. So, how did Vespucci come to have a continent named after him? In short, by way of a lie that got lucky.

In 1504–5, letters titled Mundus Novus ("New World") began circulating in Florence. The letters were forgeries but were attributed to Vespucci, stating that he had not only been the captain of his voyages but had discovered the New World. Elsewhere, Vespucci had written factually about his travels, but because the forgeries included sensational material about the sexual and dietary habits of the natives, they became very popular. Meanwhile, in France, Martin Waldseemüller was creating a new map of the world. Using the forged Vespucci letters as his source, he named the newly described landmass after the Florentine. By the time Waldseemüller learned that Vespucci was not the pioneer the letters claimed him to be, and removed Vespucci's name from his subsequent maps, the name "America" had already begun to take hold.

Despite the Americas being named after him, Amerigo Vespucci neither discovered the continents nor led the voyages in which he sailed to the New World.

THE SPANISH INROADS

As in South America, the Spanish ventured into North America in search of silver and gold. They would be disappointed. What little gold a pioneer called Hernando de Soto found among the natives in Florida had, he failed to realize, been taken by them from earlier Spanish shipwrecks. Repeatedly, Native Americans fed the Spanish dream of a northern El Dorado located "just a few more days" away. Perhaps this was their way of getting rid of the troublesome Spanish and passing them on to a neighbor.

De Soto, who was rich from expeditions among the Incas, had landed at Tampa Bay in 1539 with 500 soldiers, dozens of horses, and war dogs (mastiffs and Irish wolfhounds), along with hundreds of pigs to eat. It was his good fortune to encounter Juan Ortiz, a survivor from an earlier expedition who had been living among the Native Americans for 12 years. Ortiz would be an interpreter, along with kidnapped Native Americans, as De Soto crossed the southeast in search of booty. At times they abducted village chiefs, demanding ransom in food, women, and slaves. But as word spread about De Soto, resistance grew. In 1540 his force was attacked by the chiefdom of Tazcaluza: 22 Spaniards were killed and 148 wounded, while about 1,000 Native Americans died. Becoming more brutal after this, De Soto's forces attacked and plundered villages. However, wintering among the Chickasaws in northern Mississippi in 1541, low on supplies and not having found any riches, the decision was made to return to Mexico. Soon after that, De Soto died, and, after building boats and setting off down the Mississippi River, his men were further attacked by hundreds of Native Americans. Alive but with no bounty, the survivors made it back to Mexico City in 1543.

De Soto's expedition was just one of many throughout the sixteenth century that explored the South. Inflicting great damage, the explorers also suffered from disease and conflict with Native American tribes. Attacked by New Mexico's Acoma Pueblo Native Americans in 1598, Juan de Oñate saw his nephew's body thrown off a cliff. Deciding to make an example of his enemy, De Oñate not only killed hundreds in open battle but, following Spanish practice at the time, cut one foot off each of the adult-male prisoners.

The Spanish did succeed in establishing the town of San Agustín in Florida in 1565, and missions led by Franciscan friars were built where missionaries set about trying to develop peaceful relations with the tribes. The Spanish also often took Native American wives. The situation remained precarious, however, and by the early 1600s the Guale Native Americans were in revolt, and the Spanish in retreat. By 1706, only San Agustín and a few villages survived under Spanish control in Florida.

Leading the first European expedition to venture deep into what today is the United States, Hernando de Soto and his men tortured villagers in their fruitless search for gold in Florida. In response, the Native Americans became increasingly belligerent toward the Spanish.

THE PUEBLO REVOLT

In converting some Native Americans to Christianity, the Spanish created a new division among Native Americans, and, during the seventeenth century, there were frequent raids in New Mexico from the Apache and Navajo on Christianized Pueblo Native Americans. Later, suffering from a drought and under threat from other tribes, the Pueblo lost heart in their Christian rituals and returned to their old faith. The Franciscans' response was to arrest 47 Pueblo spiritual healers, executing three in 1675 for witchcraft, while the rest were flogged and briefly imprisoned. Five years later, the Pueblo revolted, directing their ire against 21 priests and missionaries, whom they killed, along with 380 other Spaniards.

Churches were destroyed and Pueblo religious leaders, in a reversal of baptism, bathed Christianized Native Americans in rivers to wash away the stain of Christianity.

After that, Spanish communities retreated to Mexico. It would be 16 years before the Spanish recovered New Mexico. When

IT WOULD BE 16 YEARS BEFORE THE SPANISH RECOVERED NEW MEXICO.

they returned, they did so with greater humility, no longer trying to impose their religion and culture with force, and accepting a cultural compromise. Despite all their efforts, however, the colonies of Florida, New Mexico, and Texas remained large but isolated outposts for Spain.

THE FRENCH

While the Spanish pushed into North America from the Gulf of Mexico, the French approached from the northeast, establishing a settlement on the St. Lawrence River in 1541. Although quickly abandoned, the settlers did give a name to the St. Lawrence region: they called it "Canada" after a local Native American word for "village."

For the rest of the century, the French resorted to fishing expeditions and bartering with the Native Americans in the Gulf of the St. Lawrence. Then, in the early seventeenth century, when trade was secure enough, they built a trading post—Quebec—from where French fur traders established alliances with Native American tribes, particularly the Huron. This, though, made them enemies of the Huron's own enemies, the Five Nation Iroquois. The Iroquois, in turn, allied with and secured arms from France's enemies, the Dutch, who had settled further south. In this way, both Europeans and Native Americans took advantage of the others' allegiances and hostilities.

By 1650, New France had a population of only 657, while over the same period New England had grown to 33,000. Situated more northerly, New France had a harsher climate than New England, and the taxes to be paid from the colony to the home country discouraged many from settling. So, although the French had claims on land from the Gulf of St. Lawrence down to the Gulf of Mexico by the early eighteenth century, New France remained a weaker territory than its rivals.

THE ENGLISH

What distinguished the English colonies from the Spanish and French was their relative autonomy, the opportunity of property ownership, and the benefit of excellent farming land, although their initial efforts were not promising. The first settlement, at Roanoke Island, North Carolina, in the 1580s, quickly disappeared, and the Jamestown settlement in 1607 in Virginia was nearly wiped out by starvation. One man, as the settlement's Captain John Smith reported, "did kill his wife, powdered her [with salt], and had eaten part of her before it was known." Once discovered, he was executed.

OFFICIAL SCENIC HISTORIC MARKER

TAOS CANYON

In 1692, after having been driven from New Mexico by the Pueblo Revolt of 1680, the Spanish began to re-establish their rule. In one of the last battles of the reconquest, in September 1696, Governor Diego de Vargas defeated the Indians of Taos Pueblo at nearby Taos Canyon.

The Taos Canyon in New Mexico was the scene of the 1680 revolt by Pueblo Native Americans against the Spanish settlers. Four hundred settlers were killed and the remaining 4,000 were driven out of the province.

Like the Spanish in Florida, the English had arrived in Virginia with the hope of finding gold, and also of navigating a passage through the continent to Asia. Instead, there was no gold and they soon proved that they weren't capable of feeding themselves. Help came from the local Powhatan Native Americans, but the tribe's goodwill was soon tested. By 1620, the colonists were taking land from the Powhatans without any attempt at payment. This led, in 1622, to the Powhatans killing 347 settlers—more than a quarter of the colony. Following further disputes, in 1644 the Powhatans butchered a further 400 colonists in a single day.

It might seem surprising that the Native Americans, who had no guns unless they had obtained them from Europeans, could inflict such losses on the English. However, a skilled bowman could fire six well-aimed arrows a minute, whereas someone wielding a musket could, at best, fire it three times a minute. Even then, the aim was uncertain at distance, and the musket often liable to malfunction.

A late seventeenth-century map of North America, showing how well the eastern seaboard had been mapped. In contrast, territory west of the Mississippi River is described as a "tract of land full of wild bulls."

CANOEING DOWN THE MISSISSIPPI

A major change in France's fortunes came with René-Robert Cavelier, Sieur de La Salle, a lapsed Jesuit turned explorer. With a troop of

Frenchmen and Native Americans, he established forts in the Great Lakes before, in 1682, canoeing down the Mississippi River to the Gulf of Mexico—although this was not the destination he was seeking. He'd been hoping to find a route to the Pacific and so on to Asia, but he claimed the new territory for France, anyway, naming it Louisiana after his king, Louis XIV.

La Salle's next expedition from France approached America from the Gulf of Mexico. After a troubled voyage that saw three of his four ships lost, he landed too far west; his men then spent three years trying to find the mouth of the Mississippi. In 1687, with no end in sight, his troops mutinied and shot him. A sorry end, but today La Salle's achievements as an explorer are commemorated across France, Canada and the US.

Explorer René-Robert Cavelier, Sieur de La Salle, claims possession of the Mississippi region, naming it "Louisiana" after his king, Louis XIV.

TOBACCO

A SKILLED BOWMAN COULD FIRE SIX WELL-AIMED ARROWS A MINUTE.

Although the English had not found gold in Virginia, they had come across a palatable strain of tobacco smoked by the Native Americans, which, when business took off, sold in England for up to ten times what it cost to produce in the colony. The problem was securing sufficient manpower to farm it. While in New France the difficulty was attracting migrants, in Virginia the trouble was keeping them alive. Between 1607 and 1624, about 7,600 people had emigrated from England to Virginia, but, after almost 20 years, Virginia's English population was still only about 1,200, with disease killing off many of the settlers. The local Native American population, too, was being depleted through disease, as well as being driven away in the land grab.

VIRGINIANS DEFENDING THEMSELVES AGAINST INDIANS

Despite having guns, the Europeans could still be overrun by the Native Americans. Unlike a bow and arrow, a musket could, at best, be fired three times a minute, while its aim was uncertain at a distance.

Indentured servants were introduced to work on the farms. Given a free passage to Virginia from England, the workers contracted themselves to a master for seven years. After that, they were free to work as wage earners, and, if they saved enough money, to buy their own land—something easier to achieve in Virginia than in Europe. Not that life was easy: in the early years the chance of survival for indentured servants was 50 percent.

Nor were things getting any easier. With the end of the English Civil War (1642–51), wages rose in the old country and emigration to Virginia became less appealing, while attempts at using captive Native Americans to work the fields proved unsuccessful, too. Knowing the terrain better than the English, the local tribespeople could easily escape, and enslaving a population with whom the English also needed to trade was poor for business relations. Therefore, the plantation owners looked to how manpower shortages had been resolved in another English colony in Barbados: African slave labor.

The English settlers did not find gold in Virginia, but the Native Americans did introduce them to tobacco. Cultivating it for export to the European market proved to be the making of the colony.

SLAVERY

Virginia and the Carolinas became England's first slave colonies in America. In the very early years, slaves were treated as indentured servants and were freed after completing the years of their terms. In a rather extreme example, for instance, in 1651 former slave Anthony Johnson owned 250 acres of land and had slaves of his own.

Over time, however, conditions for the slaves became harsher and more rigid. In 1662, Virginia adopted the principle that the children of slave mothers were also slaves, regardless of paternity. Following this, in 1705 the colony formalized its slave code, identifying slaves as those "who were not Christians in their native country," forbidding intermarriage with slaves, and freeing a master of punishment should he accidentally kill a slave whom he had to discipline. Whipping and violence were common, and workers would be pushed to keep up with the rate set by the fastest laborer.

Violence was the lubricant of the entire slave system. Slaves could be whipped for suspected minor thefts or for trying to run away. To make their bondage more bearable, slaves would deliberately misunderstand orders, feign ignorance, or work slowly.

Slave numbers grew rapidly. In 1680, there were roughly 4,000 people of African descent in Maryland and Virginia; 30 years later, there were 31,000. That said, in the 1730s in Virginia, only about 30 percent of slaves lived on plantations where there were 10 or more slaves; more frequently, there were only a couple of slaves per plantation. Consequently, slaves lived closely with the plantation owner and white servants. It was their status as much as their color that defined them, as historian Ira Berlin writes: "Throughout the 17th century and into the first decades of the 18th century, black and white servants ran away together, slept together, and upon occasion, stood shoulder to shoulder against… established authority."

Some slave owners raped their slaves or used them as sexual playthings, but, in South Carolina at

SOME SLAVE OWNERS RAPED THEIR SLAVES OR USED THEM AS SEXUAL PLAYTHINGS.

least, the situation became more nuanced: the more integrated lives of slaves and slaveholders meant that the holders were more inclined to recognize their sexual relations with black slave women and sometimes free the offspring of these unions from slavery. From this emerged a free caste of light-skinned people of color.

THE ATLANTIC SLAVE TRADE

Between 1700 and 1775, 250,000 African slaves were transported to North America, making up about 6 percent of all the slaves shipped across the Atlantic—far more were transported to the Caribbean and Brazil. Although it doesn't lessen the barbarity of the Atlantic slave trade, there were probably as many slaves—between three and five million—held within Africa by Africans as there were in the Americas.

Slaves were acquired through raids, through African tribal chiefs selling their captives and prisoners of war, and from African slave traders. Onboard ships, the captives were chained at the

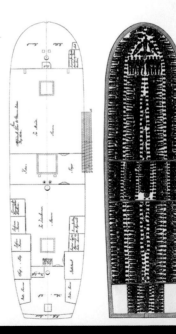

The deck plan of a slave ship in the 1700s. With around 200 slaves shackled closely together, slave ships developed a stink that could be smelled miles downwind.

neck and stacked on wooden shelves about 30 inches (75 cm) high. Lying in their own excrement and urine, many died of dysentery. Some starved themselves to death, while others tried to jump overboard when brought on deck for food and exercise. Occasionally there were rebellions on board—even more occasionally these were successful.

Conditions improved during the eighteenth century as crossing times were reduced by a few weeks to no more than two months; by the 1780s, nine out of 10 slaves were surviving the voyage.

A NEW ENGLAND

The *Mayflower* may be romantically remembered as the beginning of New England, but within a year of arriving half its 102 passengers were dead. Even so, as families of artisans and craftsmen, largely unused to

THE STONO REBELLION

In contrast with British colonies, slavery in Spanish Florida was usually less harsh: there, slaves often had the right to marry and to hold property—and the territory welcomed runaways from other parts of the East Coast. With this in mind, in 1739, 20 slaves at Stono Bridge, near Charles Town (Charleston), South Carolina, stole guns and began marching towards Florida.

Attacking plantations and killing more than 20 colonists along the way, their numbers soon swelled to around a hundred. But within a day, the plantation owners had caught up with them, shot them, and, just as the rebels had done to some of the whites, decapitated many.

Often in the slave states, this was more complicated than just a case of black against white: 30 slaves, mainly assimilated Creoles, had remained loyal to their white masters and had killed some of the black insurgents.

Although swiftly dealt with, the Stono Rebellion sent shock waves through the white population in South Carolina, which was outnumbered two-to-one by its slaves. Consequently, slave laws were tightened.

Unlike other early settlers, the Pilgrim Fathers were not seeking commercial gain in America, but a promised land where they would be free to practice their religion.

working the land, they were lucky in that the local Wampanoag tribe helped them, particularly a member of the Wampanoag they called Squanto. New England was not completely unchartered territory. Having been taken from the coast by English fishermen, Squanto had spent 15 years abroad, some of that time working in London, and some in slavery in Spain, before returning home on another exploratory expedition. He was a good man for the newcomers to know.

Unlike the gold-seekers in the South, the first settlers in New England in 1620 had been primarily motivated by religion—they were Separatists from the Church of England. Believing Judgment was nearing, John Winthrop, a Puritan who led the first large wave of immigrants to New England 10 years later, proclaimed: "God hathe provided this place [New England] to be a refuge for manye whom he meanes to save." New England, they believed, was destined for them, and they were not going to tolerate dissenters: accordingly, they hanged several Quakers who repeatedly tried to proselytize, and they excommunicated Anne Hutchinson for preaching, banishing her from Massachusetts in 1638.

Although New England did not become a major slave-owning colony, that wasn't down to the Puritans' faith, but because tobacco and rice didn't grow in the cooler northern climate—so there was no need for such a large workforce as there was on the plantations in the South. Some slaves worked as farm laborers and domestic servants in New England, although, at most, in Rhode Island in 1710, they made up only 5 percent of the population. In contrast, by 1775 in Virginia, two out of five people were black slaves.

The attack by English, Narragansett, and Mohegan forces against Pequot men, women, and children in New England in 1637. Many of the Native Americans not killed in the Pequot War (1636–38) were sold into slavery in the West Indies.

SCALPING

Warring Native Americans had long taken scalps as battlefield trophies, but it was the Europeans who turned scalping into a business. As an indication of the hostility between the colonies and the Native Americans, and also among tribes themselves, scalp bounties began appearing in the 1670s. Lacking much of an army, Massachusetts paid £10 per scalp to scalp hunters during Queen Anne's War in 1702, while during the 1711 war with the Tuscarora in North Carolina, John Barnwell led an expedition that scalped 52 Native Americans, including 10 women. But scalping worked the other way, too: during the French and Indian War, the French offered bounties for British scalps.

New England may have been founded on Puritan spirit, but, as the story of Hannah Dustan demonstrates, it proved to be a brutal frontier. In 1698, an Abenaki war party captured Dustan, along with her newborn child and her nurse, Mary Neff, in Haverhill, Massachusetts. The following day, one of the Abenaki warriors killed Dustan's baby, before forcing her and Neff to join another warrior, along with Abenaki women and children, on a 150-mile (240-km) trek towards Canada. After some days, Dustan took a tomahawk from a sleeping Abenaki and, with the help of Neff and a teenage boy who had been captured, crushed the skulls of the Abenaki men. Dustan didn't stop there. She scalped her victims and others in the war party, later presenting the Massachusetts General Assembly with 10 scalps—for which she was rewarded £50.

By embracing scalp hunting, writes historian John Grenier, American society had not only commercialized war, but "made the killing of non-combatants a legitimate act of war."

An American propaganda cartoon from the 1812 war with Britain, criticizing the "humane" British and their "worthy" Native American allies who scalp Americans.

Not only were there fewer slaves in the North compared with the South, they had better rights, too, not being classified as property in Massachusetts, and, following conversion to Christianity in New Amsterdam, in some cases they were given their freedom. When New Amsterdam was acquired by England in 1664, 75 of the town's 375 blacks were free.

MASSACHUSETTS PAID £10 PER SCALP TO SCALP HUNTERS DURING QUEEN ANNE'S WAR IN 1702.

NATIVE AMERICAN REVOLTS AND REBELLIONS

The arrival of Europeans seldom prompted unity among Indian tribes against a common enemy. With tension building between the Puritans and Indians in New England in the 1630s, the Pequot Indians sought an alliance with the Narragansetts. But rather than seizing an opportunity for Indian solidarity, the Narragansetts saw a chance to remove a rival tribe: they sided with the English.

The most notable event of the Pequot War (1636–48) was the 1637 attack by English, Narragansett, and Mohegan forces on Fort Mystic. Most of the Pequot warriors were away raiding English settlements, but this didn't stop the English-led force setting fire to the fort and killing the women, children, and old men who tried to escape. It is estimated that around 600 Pequots died in the attack; the Puritans lost two people.

Two months later, when the English defeated the remaining Pequot, their chief, Sassacus, fled to Mohawk territory, where he was beheaded. The Mohawks weren't going to involve themselves in the war or side with non-Iroquoian people. Meanwhile, the remaining Pequots were sold into slavery in Bermuda or divided up among the Narragansetts and Mohegans as payment. As a political force in the seventeenth century, the Pequot were extinguished, as the Narragansetts had hoped—not that they would last much longer, either.

When the English executed three Wampanoag men for murdering a Christianized Indian who had warned the English of a planned

Wampanoag attack, revenge attacks from the Wampanoag and other native tribes ensued. This was the first time that the Puritans had prosecuted an Indian for an Indian crime—and it led to a massacre. The English retaliated, butchering hundreds of Narragansett men, women and children—as well as English men who had Indian wives.

In 1729, the Natchez in Mississippi rebelled against French encroachments, killing more than 200 settlers. With the French military response being to sell hundreds of Natchez prisoners into slavery, by the late 1730s the tribe had ceased to exist as an independent people.

It would get worse. When Metacom, the Wampanoag chief, and his followers sought help from the Iroquois, the Iroquois attacked them, while the Mohegans backed the English. In August 1676, the English caught Metacom, decapitating him. His wife and hundreds of survivors were sold into slavery in the West Indies. With 3000 Indians killed in the short war (600 English died), the Wampanoags and Narragansetts were virtually exterminated.

This treatment wasn't limited to the English. In the South in 1729, Natchez Indians rebelled with slaves, freeing other slaves and killing more than 200 French settlers—almost all the French men in the area.

Unusually, Pontiac's Rebellion in 1763 saw Native Americans uniting against the Europeans. In the uprising, a loose confederation of northern Native American tribes captured nine British forts and attacked ships on the Detroit River.

In response, the French sent slaves and Choctaw Indians against the Natchez, massacring hundreds and selling the Natchez survivors into slavery. By 1736, the few remaining Natchez had dispersed to live among the Cherokee and Cree. As with many conflicts between Europeans and Indians, the French had managed to exploit local enmities and employ one tribe of Indians against another.

Thirty years later, one rebellion would prove the exception to this rule. In Pontiac's Rebellion, northern tribes united in a large pan-Indian movement against the British, capturing nine British forts and besieging Detroit for three years. Finally crushing the rebellion, the British took the uprising seriously enough to issue a proclamation to the colonists to remain east of the Appalachians to avoid further conflict. This, though, wasn't respected, and tensions between the colonists and Indians would remain high.

THE SALEM WITCH TRIALS

Up until 1692, a total of 12 women had been hanged as witches in Massachusetts and Connecticut, but in the period between February 1692 and May 1693, 20 people were executed for witchcraft in or around Salem, Massachusetts. Another 156 were imprisoned. What was going on? Probably nothing more satanic, but no less sinister, than mass hysteria.

Most accusations of witchcraft in New England at that time were dismissed, but when in Salem Village (present-day Danvers), Betty Paris, nine, and her cousin, Abigail Williams, 11, fell ill with convulsions and screaming fits, and no medical cause could be found, people began to wonder if the children were under a magic spell. Three years earlier, there had been a case in Boston of children convulsing and accusations of witchcraft, of which the people of Salem would have been aware.

By now the two girls had been joined by two more cases of convulsions: 12-year-old Ann Putnam and Elizabeth Hubbard, who was probably 17. Pressed to reveal their tormentors, the girls described how witches had appeared to them in spirit form and had caused the convulsions.

The first women to be accused of witchcraft were, unsurprisingly for witch trials, three social outsiders: Tituba, a slave who was either black or Native American; Sarah Good, a beggar known to curse those who crossed her; and Sarah Osborne, a woman who had damned herself in the eyes of the community by living with a man before marrying.

But, rather than remaining limited to these three suspects, the accusations grew. More suspects were hauled into court, where they usually confessed to protect themselves and named accomplices, thus fueling the hysteria. The accusations spread from Salem to neighboring Andover, and although new colonial magistrates were sent for, in the hope of throwing cold water on the matter, they, too, believed the girls' testimonies and further fanned the flames.

Twenty people were executed in the Salem witch trials of 1692–93 before the accusations of witchcraft began to be doubted and the mass hysteria was extinguished.

By May 1692, 62 people were in custody. With any sense of justice temporarily abandoned, if the accused refused to admit any guilt, he or she was found guilty anyway and executed. Sarah Good, whose four-year-old daughter even gave evidence as a prosecution witness, was hanged. Sarah Osborne, whom Good accused of being a witch, died in prison. Tituba, who confessed under trial, was imprisoned but released after the scare had passed.

Meanwhile, the accusations climbed the social ranks, reaching Mary Phips, the wife of Massachusetts's Governor Phips. But when Samuel Willard, pastor of the First Church of Boston and president of Harvard University, was accused, the magistrates' credulity snapped.

Beginning to doubt all the testimony they had heard, the magistrates dismissed the girls' evidence, and the governor called a new hearing. Fifty-two people were retried, only three of whom were found guilty—and they were reprieved, along with all those already in prison.

Of the 20 who had been executed, 19 had been hanged, and one, Giles Corey, was gradually tortured to death by being crushed by ever-heavier stones in an attempt to make him offer a plea.

Whether the girls were attention-seeking frauds, affected by a kind of social epidemic following the incident in Boston, or afflicted with a psychological or physical illness, is not known. Successive generations of historians have offered varying theories for what happened in Salem. Was it about class, gender, rivalry among Puritan families, or an expression of the violence felt from the wars with Native Americans? Or was it a combination of all these factors at that time that allowed the mania to take hold?

CONVICTS

Of the 80,000 English migrants to America between 1700 and 1775, around 50,000 of them were convicts. Not only did transporting criminals put them out of sight and mind of the authorities, but there was plenty of work to be done in the colonies' plantations. Most convicts were young, male, unskilled laborers who had been found guilty of theft, but those sentenced to death in England for murder could petition the king and might, if they were lucky, receive a transportation pardon.

While most transported criminals were thieves or had been found guilty of violent crime, in 1732 inmates from Britain's debtors' prisons—including members of the aristocracy—were sent to Georgia.

As on slave ships, convicts were chained at the neck for most of the journey, although they had slightly more space than slaves. Once in the colonies, they were sold. "They searched us there as the dealers in horses do those animals," remembered convict William Green, "looking at our teeth, viewing our limbs, to see if they are sound and fit for their labor." Convicts sold at a third the price of adult male slaves and could be worked for more years than indentured servants. Whippings were commonplace, as were iron collars and chains, if the convict was considered unruly.

As criminals they arrived, but as historian A. Roger Ekirch has noted, convicts in America "committed surprisingly few crimes." There were cases of runaways, some even making it back to Britain, but after most had served their terms, the men usually moved to a new neighborhood in an effort to distance themselves from the stigma of their servitude. Then they could try to begin a new life.

The Battle of Quebec in September 1759 was not quite the decisive triumph remembered by the British. Although quickly victorious, the British garrison was subsequently marooned in the city, the starving, disease-ridden survivors only being rescued the following spring.

EUROPE'S WAR IN AMERICA

In the eighteenth century, British colonies were surging ahead in wealth and population, with settlers from Virginia and Pennsylvania starting to expand into the Ohio Valley. This area reached from the Appalachians up to the Great Lakes, and, although largely unoccupied by Europeans, it had long been claimed as part of New France. So, in response to the British encroachment (Great Britain having formally

> **TO FIGHT IN AMERICA, THE BRITISH AND FRENCH NEEDED THE HELP OF THE LOCAL NATIVE AMERICANS.**

come into existence in 1707 with the Act of Union between the kingdoms of England and Scotland), the French began building a chain of forts from Lake Erie down to Fort Duquesne (present-day Pittsburgh).

By 1754, the two European powers were at war over Ohio County, a part of a broader global conflict between Britain and France, and their allies, in the French and Indian War (1756–63). To fight in America, both the British and French needed the help of the local Native Americans. A confederacy of Iroquois tribes had kept a peaceful alliance with the French in the Ohio County, but the British now disrupted this by drawing the Mohawks away.

George Washington (*on horseback*) during the French and Indian War. One outcome of the war determined whether the people of North America would mainly speak English or French.

French forces based at Fort Duquesne defeated the English in 1754 and also in 1755, when the English ranks of conspicuous redcoats were easily picked off by French and Native American troops unseen in the trees. Worse was to come in a botched assault on Fort Carillon

(Ticonderoga) on the Hudson River three years later. It would be the bloodiest battle in this conflict (also known as the Seven Years' War) with 1,000 losses on the British side. In 1758, the British succeeded in taking the now-abandoned Fort Duquesne, only to find a line of stakes each topped with the skull of a British soldier—a grim reminder of their earlier defeat.

THE BATTLE OF QUEBEC

The key to French America was the fort at Quebec, which stands 300 ft (91 m) above the St. Lawrence River. It is popularly remembered—in Britain, at least—that although the fort was near impregnable, the British, under General James Wolfe, managed a swift, surprising victory. By scaling a steep path at night, the British engaged the French on the Plains of Abraham and eliminated them with just two volleys. Within 10 minutes, the battle was over.

If that sounds too good to be true, it is. In fact, there were two battles at Quebec: Wolfe's victory in September 1759 was succeeded by a more decisive one the following year. But first, the 7,000 British troops who had conquered the city now had to survive the winter where food shortages led to scurvy. By the spring, when 7,000 refreshed French forces headed down the St. Lawrence, there were only 3,000 British troops who were battle worthy.

Again the troops met on the Plains of Abraham, but this time the battle was not resolved quickly. After two hours of hand-to-hand combat, half the British were dead or wounded, and the able-bodied were fleeing back behind the city walls.

IN THE SPACE OF JUST OVER 250 YEARS, EUROPEANS HAD COLONIZED EASTERN AMERICA.

Still unresolved, Quebec was not won by the British until the main fleet arrived the following month and the French retreated. By the end of the year, all the French forts were in British hands.

The battle had been fought over land, but it was sea power that settled the victory. By 1763, the French and Indian War was over, New France formally becoming part of the British colonies. In an act of eighteenth-century ethnic cleansing, 7,000 French-Canadian settlers were deported from Nova Scotia down to France's remaining colony at Louisiana. However, France's hand in the future of America was not over yet.

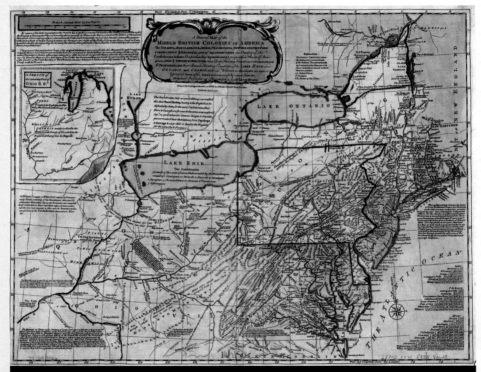

This 1771 map of the middle British colonies was designed to spur westward expansion following French encroachments. Its text warns that George III risks losing "one of the best gems in his Crown to [French] usurpation and boundless ambition!"

THE NEW WORLD

In the space of just over 250 years, Europeans had colonized eastern America, decimating the Native American population through disease and war and dispossessing a great many. Along with convicts from Britain, the Europeans had brought thousands of slaves from Africa, and fought their own imperial wars over American territory. But the colonies were now a major part of Atlantic trade, and the more successful and established they became, the more they prized their importance, and, in time, their independence.

With the fall of New France, members of the British colonies had celebrated by erecting statues to Britain's King George III and his leading politician, William Pitt. Yet within 12 years, the colonists would be at war with Britain—the war that would create the United States.

Although a veteran of the French and Indian War, George Washington was not highly experienced in battle before becoming commander in chief of the Continental Army.

CHAPTER 2

THE AMERICAN REVOLUTION

WHAT BEGAN IN 1765 AS A TAX DISPUTE WITH BRITAIN ESCALATED through war to see the United States emerge as an independent nation. But, although the infant republic embraced ideals of liberty and equality, it would refuse to extend these rights to its slaves and its Native Americans.

The French and Indian War (1756–63) had not just doubled Britain's national debt, it had also made running the 13 colonies of North America five times more expensive. For this, London wanted to make the colonists pay their share, particularly because Great Britain was now keeping a standing army in North America. What followed between 1763 and 1776 was a series of efforts by Britain to extract revenue from the American colonies—a plan that was countered by increasingly violent resistance by colonists on the grounds that they shouldn't pay taxes if they were not represented at Parliament in London. As the famous slogan went: "No taxation with representation."

Not that representation was widely given in Britain, either. At the time, only around one in six adult British males had the right to vote, compared with two in three in the American colonies. Indeed, Britain's electoral districts were an unreformed, corrupt hodgepodge that allowed districts with barely any inhabitants a representative at Parliament while new cities such as Manchester had none.

But then, just as electoral reform in Britain lagged behind population change, so the country's management of its colonies was also out of touch. In 1700, the population of the American colonies had been one-twentieth the size of that of Britain and Ireland combined; by 1770, however, it was a fifth—2.1 million compared with more than 10 million in the British Isles. However, apart from efforts to extract taxes, London did not treat these rapidly emerging people any differently than it had always done. To London, the American colonies, like other parts of the empire, were unsophisticated, lesser entities. Showing its lack of consideration for American opinion, Parliament passed the Quebec Act in 1774, granting freedom of worship for Catholics in the largely French-speaking territories, ceded to Britain by the Treaty of Paris in 1763, and giving the governor of Quebec control over the vast Native American lands of the Ohio Valley. Enlightened though it may have been in its attitude towards the defeated French population, the Quebec Act managed to provoke American Protestants, land speculators, and traders.

SONS OF LIBERTY AND BOSTON TEA

In March 1765, the British Parliament approved a stamp duty on legal documents and newspapers in the American colonies. Distinct from duties on trade, this was the first "direct" tax introduced to the colonies—and it was resisted. In August that year, leaders of the opposition to the Stamp Act roused Boston's city mobs. Having, it was said, plied them with drink, they sent them against representatives of the British government, a riot that included the ransacking of the house of the lieutenant-governor of Massachusetts.

Rioting then spread across the 13 colonies, led not by thugs but mostly by middle-ranking people—mechanics, small merchants, and shopkeepers—who commonly called themselves "Sons of Liberty." Having blocked imports of British goods, the protests died down only when London repealed the Stamp Act the following February.

In June 1767, Charles Townshend, the British Chancellor of the Exchequer, tried a different method of extracting more revenue out of the colonies by imposing higher duties on glass, paper, and tea. Once more, this met resistance from local committees, with boycotts placed on British goods in return. Despite voices in Parliament arguing that using force would undermine any goodwill with Americans, more troops were sent from Britain to be garrisoned in Boston. By 1769, there were nearly 4,000 British soldiers in a town of 15,000 people. Then, in March 1770, in a clash involving a mob that had harassed soldiers, five civilians were killed—the first fatalities in the developing conflict.

The protests and resistance had proved their point. With the little revenue collected by the Townshend Duties far overshadowed by the loss in trade through boycotts, the duties were largely repealed.

Britain, however, still didn't see the danger it was provoking. When, in May 1773, it disregarded American merchants' concerns and gave the ailing East India Company a monopoly to sell tea in North America, protests soon followed. The most remarkable of these has become known as the Boston Tea Party. On December 16, 1773, a group of 60 men, including apprentices, sailors and merchants—some vaguely disguised as Native Americans—dumped 340 chests of newly imported tea into Boston Harbor.

The British immediately responded with the Intolerable Acts (or Coercive Acts) of 1774, putting Boston under martial law, closing the port, and assert-ing greater authority over local appointments. This worked in the protesters' favor, as the colonies began

THE NOTION OF INDEPENDENCE WAS NOW BEING DISCUSSED IN COLONIAL NEWSPAPERS.

to unite against Britain by sending donations to Boston. For the first time, the notion of independence was being discussed in colonial newspapers.

"Unhappy Boston! See thy sons deplore, thy hallowed walks besmeared with guiltless gore," begins Paul Revere's propaganda poster "The Bloody Massacre," which reported the shooting by the British Army of five civilians in Boston in March 1770.

THE CONTINENTAL CONGRESS

Openly rebelling, the colonies now pushed aside royal authority and allowed new local administrators to levy taxes, supervise courts, and organize militias. Meeting in Philadelphia, a Continental Congress of around 50 men from 12 colonies (Georgia didn't take part) discussed the colonies' future, agreeing to block imports from Britain, but holding in reserve a ban of exports to Britain that would have ruined the economy in the South. Most delegates, though, still hoped for reconciliation with the mother country.

There were voices of support in London, too, such as that of Edward Burke, MP, who called for the Americans to be represented at Parliament and for a relaxing of the tax legislation. The prevailing opinion there, however, was for punishing the upstart colonies.

"The rebels are not the despicable rabble too many have supposed them to be," wrote British commander George Gage after his victory at Bunker Hill in June 1775 had cost him 250 men.

FROM LEXINGTON TO BUNKER HILL

On April 19, 1775, a force of British soldiers from Boston marched into the village of Lexington, Massachusetts, in search of illegal arms. They were confronted by 70 local militiamen, a shot rang out—it's not clear from which side—and the British charged, killing eight Americans within a few minutes. Moving on to Concord the same day, the British didn't find any guns, but the town was set ablaze anyway. Then, while returning the 16-mile (26-km) journey to Boston, they were attacked. By the end of the day, 70 British soldiers had been killed and 200 wounded; on the colonists' side the wounded or dead totaled 95. Worse was to come. Two months later, the British dislodged the colonists fortifying Bunker Hill outside Boston, but it cost them 250 lives and a further 750 wounded. With the fighting escalating, the Continental Congress decided to create a Continental Army with George Washington as commander.

THE UNITED STATES OF COLUMBIA

What, though, were the 13 colonies going to call their new nation? The Declaration of Independence had stated "The Unanimous Declaration of the Thirteen United States of America," and, that same year, Thomas Paine in *Common Sense*, his influential book arguing for independence, had first referred to "the United States of America." There was, however, some hesitation in Congress, particularly because the word "America" could, they thought, refer to anyone from all the Americas, not just the 13 colonies. Congress debated the matter, even considering the name "United States of Columbia." As Columbus's voyages had been financed by the Spanish crown, his reputation in the 13 colonies had not been cultivated by the British and his name had faded. But when the colonies began to look for new figureheads separate from Britain, his reputation saw a revival.

In the end, Congress decided to embrace the word "America," leaving Columbus to live on in the names of US colleges, territories, towns and cities.

THE DECLARATION OF INDEPENDENCE

While moderates were still calling for representation in Parliament, in June 1776, John Adams, a Boston lawyer active in the protests, and Richard

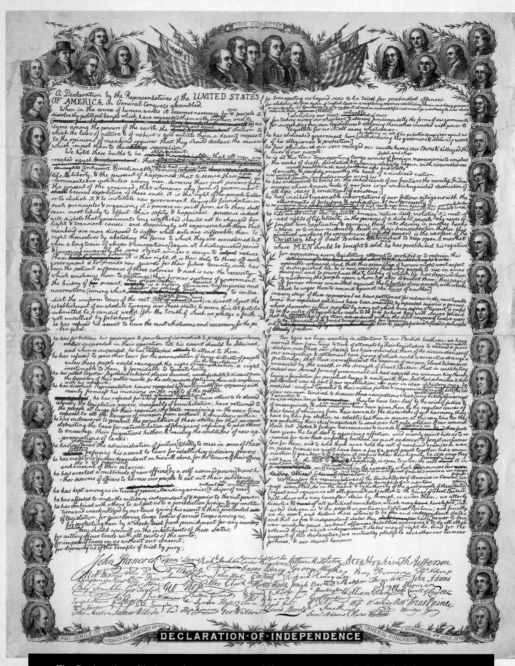

The Declaration of Independence pronounced that governments derive "their just powers from the consent of the governed," and that, as the British were seeking "an absolute tyranny," the political connection between the United States and Britain was dissolved.

Henry Lee of Virginia, proposed a resolution in the Congress: "That these United States are, and of right ought to be, free and independent States, and that they are absolved from all allegiance to the British Crown.…"

Approving the motion, the Continental Congress appointed Thomas Jefferson, a committee member from Virginia, to draft a formal declaration of independence. While holding King George III accountable for all of America's grievances, the final 1,300-word Declaration is very much an expression of the Enlightenment ideals of its day: "We hold these truths to be self-evident; that all men are created equal; that they are endowed by their Creator with certain inalienable rights; that among these are life, liberty and the pursuit of happiness.…" The equality and liberty of white men, that is. In their eyes, women and slaves were not equal.

On July 4, 1776, the Continental Congress approved the Declaration of Independence. John Adams wrote to his wife Abigail that Independence Day "will be celebrated by succeeding generations as the great annual festival." He was right. Where 13 years earlier statues of George III had been erected across the colonies after the victory in the French and Indian War, now the king's effigy was torn down.

THE ARMIES

Independence might have been declared, but now the colonists had to realize it by breaking away from the world's most powerful nation. In 1776 alone, Britain sent 30,000 troops to North America, whereas the Continental Army usually numbered fewer than 5,000 men, supplemented by state militia. After a season, America's soldiers would mostly return to their farms. There was another problem, too, in that about a fifth of white Americans remained loyal to the crown, with thousands fighting on the British side. Although the Americans lacked resources, the British faced other difficulties. Their war was 3,000 miles (4,828 km) from home, and they were fighting not to crush an enemy, but to win it over. Also, America was vast and lacked a capital to conquer. As a consequence, the British efforts focused on attacking the Congress's main army, in the hope that the colonies would lose faith in the rebellion.

With a smaller and weaker army, George Washington decided to fight defensively and avoid full-scale action, relying on skirmishes to disrupt the

THEIR IDEALS OF EQUALITY AND LIBERTY DIDN'T EXTEND TO WOMEN AND SLAVES.

British supply chain. Reporting after Bunker Hill that American riflemen had concealed themselves behind trees before sneakily taking shots, one British soldier complained: "What an unfair method of carrying on a war!" Like much of the British effort, he was missing the point. "The British never really understood what they were up against," writes historian Gordon S. Wood. "Hence they continually underestimated the staying power of the rebels and overestimated the strength of the Loyalists."

REACHING SARATOGA

During the British campaign to occupy Philadelphia, George Washington was defeated twice in Pennsylvania in the autumn of 1777. However, the defeats were not disastrous and instead proved how well the Americans could stand up to superior forces. Meanwhile, a British force led by John Burgoyne had moved south from Canada in an effort to control the

WITH WAR APPROACHING, SOME SLAVES BEGAN TO SUPPORT THEIR ENEMY'S ENEMY—THE BRITISH.

Hudson River. With an overextended supply train, and following skirmishes with the colonists, his 6,000 troops found themselves surrounded by superior numbers at Saratoga, New York, and fought two small battles before surrendering.

More significant than the outcome at Saratoga was its wider impact. Encouraged by the American victory, the French, who had already secretly been supplying the Americans with money and arms, signed a

FIGHTING SLAVES

With war approaching, some slaves began to support their enemy's enemy—the British. In September 1774, Boston slaves offered to serve General Thomas Gage against their American masters; the following year, slaves in Rhode Island joined a group of Loyalists. Virginia's governor, John Murray, the Earl of Dunmore, seeing his white population turn against him, declared that he would free all slaves who were willing to fight for him. Between 800 and 1,000 slaves, including families, slipped away from their jobs and joined what Dunmore called the Ethiopian Regiment. Their military efforts were largely unsuccessful, but Dunmore managed to disperse the survivors, sending the battle-worthy ones north to join Loyalist forces in New York and the rest to friendly territory in Florida and the West Indies.

American forces try to hold their ground at Brandywine, Pennsylvania, in September 1777. With more than 14,000 troops on each side, it was the largest engagement in the Revolutionary War.

treaty with the United States, recognizing their independence and simultaneously declaring war on Britain. The Spanish and the Dutch then joined in on the French side. The 13 colonies now had major European might on their side.

HEADING SOUTH

Having failed in New England in 1777, the British turned their efforts towards the South. Charleston, South Carolina, was won in May 1780 by the British after a three-month siege—although the following year the Americans regained control of most of that area. Then Washington marched south, trapping the British on Virginia's York peninsula. Usually, the British, with the world's largest navy, had the upper hand in sea power, but here their troops on land were denied any escape because the French fleet was blockading them.

Pleading illness, British General Charles Cornwallis did not attend the surrender ceremony at Yorktown in October 1781, leaving his second-in-command, General Charles O'Hara, to carry Cornwallis's sword to the American and French commanders.

Unable to maneuver and facing a force of 17,000 to his own 8,000 troops, Lord Cornwallis was besieged at Yorktown. After three weeks, with smallpox spreading and his men beginning to starve, Cornwallis was forced to surrender. Support finally came to the British in the form of 25 ships and 7,000 men, but it arrived on the day terms were concluded.

The war wasn't over, but, writes historian Gordon S. Wood, "everyone knew that Yorktown meant American independence." Peace finally came in September 1783 with the British signing the Treaty of Paris, acknowledging the full independence of the United States.

INOCULATIONS AND MUTINIES

With a smallpox epidemic decimating the American army in 1777, George Washington stepped up what had previously been a haphazard policy of inoculations. This was 20 years before Edward Jenner in England demonstrated the use of cowpox as a form of vaccination and set the course for widespread treatment of smallpox, so Washington's efforts were rudimentary and sometimes disastrous. He had, however, little choice, and established a quarantine unit where every soldier would have some smallpox pustules from an earlier victim inserted into an incision in his arm, thus transferring a mild dose of the virus in the hope of building immunity rather than killing the patient.

Apart from disease, the American soldiers often struggled financially because Congress lacked the organization to support its soldiers and the individual states proved unwilling to group together to pay for the war. Unpaid and barely fed, several American units mutinied in the winter of 1779–80. As mutineer Joseph Martin from Connecticut explained: "The men saw no other alternative but to starve to death, or break up the army...."

THE AFTERMATH

The war was experienced very differently across the colonies: while the Carolinas and Georgia saw much of the fighting, Massachusetts's moment happened in 1776 and Virginia's with Yorktown in 1781, but both were otherwise little touched by the conflict. Slave experiences varied, too, as slaves fought on both sides. After the war, those who had been freed by the British were relocated to Canada or the West Indies, just as white Loyalists moved to Canada or Britain.

General Anthony Wayne trying to quell the Pennsylvania Line Mutiny in 1781. During the Revolutionary War, American soldiers repeatedly mutinied over lack of food or pay.

Although the war may not have seen immense battles or long campaigns, 25,000 Americans died in it—in proportion to the population, the greatest loss of life after the Civil War. Of these deaths, only a third were lost in battle, the rest dying of disease.

Unsurprisingly, the war was waged at huge financial cost to the Americans. To fund it, Congress had printed money, leading to high inflation, as well as having borrowed massively from the French and Dutch. The United States was born heavily in debt. Now unprotected by the British flag, many American ships were attacked and their crews sold into slavery by corsairs from Muslim states in North Africa. With little money to spare, Congress could not pay any ransoms or tribute. Independence may have carried great enthusiasm, but there were immense problems to be addressed.

THE CONSTITUTION

The Americans had declared their independence, and then gone on to win it. Now the Founding Fathers had to build a workable nation. During the war, each of the colonies had rewritten their constitutions as independent states, largely restricting the role of their British-sanctioned governors, and increasing the authority of local elected assemblies. The Revolution, though, hadn't only been about shaking off British tyranny, but blocking any future kind of tyranny. As property qualifications for voters were reduced, many more people became enfranchised, thus allowing farmers, merchants, and lawyers to join what had previously been the exclusive domain of wealthy gentlemen. Rule by monarchy and aristocracy was now a thing of the colonial past.

However, this could create its own problems at the other extreme, with too much power concentrated locally. Thomas Jefferson complained that when "all the powers of government, legislative, executive, and judiciary, result to the legislative body" the government in Virginia had turned "despotic." Another future president, James Madison of Virginia, said that "a spirit of locality" in the state legislatures was the states, destroying "the aggregate interests of the community."

Added to this, in their uneasy alliance, the states were fighting commercial and territorial wars among themselves, with, for example, Connecticut charging higher tariffs on goods from Massachusetts than it did on imports from Britain, New York arguing with Rhode Island over land, and Vermont already threatening to leave the union.

When, by 1787, the government was unable to repay its debts or reliably levy taxes, it was uncertain as to whether it could honor its treaty obligations or ensure that its laws would be obeyed. "It was not clear," wrote historian Charles L. Mee, "that it could be called a government at all."

In an effort to reach an agreement across the country, the Constitutional Convention met over the summer of 1787, from which emerged a national Constitution. Three major issues for the Convention were the differences in influence between small and large states, slavery, and state power versus that of a new federal government.

As small states feared that they wouldn't have a voice in a national government, a compromise was struck: while in the lower house of the legislature, a state's presence would be determined by its population—so, Rhode Island would have only a single seat, while Virginia would have 10—this would be counter-balanced in the Senate, where each state, regardless of size, would have two seats.

George Washington presiding over the Constitutional Convention in 1787. For four months, the 55 delegates debated the content of the new republic's constitution. Notably, neither John Adams nor Thomas Jefferson was present, as both were serving as US ambassadors in Europe.

On the matter of slaves, the Southern states regarded them as property and did not allow them to be part of the electorate. They did, however, count each slave as three-fifths of a person when it came to arguing the size of their population, which therefore decided how many seats they deserved in the House of Representatives. While viewed as "cruel bondage" and inhumane by many, slavery wasn't something about which the Southern states would negotiate: it had to be accepted as peculiar to them if the Constitution was to be ratified.

As for the federal government, it would have responsibility for war, diplomacy, taxation, borrowing, coining money and the regulation of trade, while its power would be controlled with a series of checks and balances. The executive, legislature, and judiciary would all be separate. Senators would be chosen by the legislature, and members of the House of Representatives by the electorate.

ALTHOUGH IT VIOLATED THE REVOLUTION'S IDEALS, ABOLISHING SLAVERY WAS UNTHINKABLE.

THE BILL OF RIGHTS

The Constitution was ratified state-by-state in 1787–88, with George Washington unanimously elected president—not by the public, but by senior figures appointed by the individual states. Still, opponents in many states, fearing a loss of basic freedoms to the national government, demanded a Bill of Rights.

Ten amendments to the Constitution were ratified in 1791. Of these, the First Amendment affirms freedom of speech and the press and that "Congress shall make no law respecting an establishment of religion," while the Tenth addresses the essential balance in the US between the federal government and the individual states, clarifying that the government possesses only those powers delegated to it by the states or the people through the Constitution.

It is the Second Amendment of these original 10 that today provokes the most emotional response. It states: "A well-regulated militia being necessary to the security of a free state, the right of the people to bear arms shall not be infringed." It would seem that in the late eighteenth century this meant citizens should own weapons and know how to use them to serve their state militia. That is no longer true today when there is a professional army, the FBI, and police forces throughout the country. Whether the Second

Amendment should be interpreted more broadly, as it is by many, to mean an individual's unconditional right to possess firearms to defend himself or herself, remains at the heart of the ongoing debate about gun control.

Addressing the objections of anti-Federalists, the Bill of Rights declares that all powers not specifically delegated to Congress are reserved for the states or the people.

SLAVERY AND LIBERTY

Shortly after arriving in America from England in 1774, Thomas Paine witnessed a slave auction in Philadelphia—the city of brotherly love.

"With what consistency of decency," he would write, could American slaveholders "complain so loudly of attempts to enslave them, while they hold so many hundred thousand in slavery?"

So how did Americans reconcile their calls for liberty on the one hand with their ownership of slaves on the other? Many, particularly in the North, did not: Vermont's 1777 constitution, for instance, called slavery a violation of "natural, inherent and inalienable rights." And, partly through conscience and partly because uncertainty in the economy favored free labor, some Philadelphia masters began to free their slaves in

Thomas Paine's pamphlet *Common Sense*, published in January 1776, was enormously influential in arguing for independence. Paine, though, wasn't from the colonies, but had arrived from England just two years earlier.

1774. The same year, the northern colonies, as well as Virginia and Carolina, banned the Atlantic slave trade at the urging of the Continental Congress.

However, even though it violated the ideals behind the Revolution—and many realized that—totally abolishing slavery was, at that time, unthinkable: it was the cornerstone of the Southern economy and all white Americans, both northern and southern, benefited from it directly or indirectly.

Also, in parts of the South where black populations were much larger, free blacks were feared. In Georgia in November 1774, six male and four female slaves were burned alive at the stake after murdering their plantation overseer, his wife, and several whites on neighboring plantations. The punishment wasn't just torturous vengeance for the crime, but a warning against other potential rebellions.

Through the continued Atlantic slave trade in some states and through children being born into slavery, there were far more blacks enslaved at the end of the Revolutionary era than at the beginning. One thing had changed, however. The Revolution had brought an end to a different era: that of slavery's unquestioned existence.

Slaves working on a cotton plantation. Slavery was the cornerstone of the Southern economy—both George Washington and Thomas Jefferson owned slaves on their Virginia plantations.

A REVOLUTION FOR NATIVE AMERICANS?

Native Americans fought on both sides in the war: the Oneidas and Tuscaroras, for instance, stayed with the Americans, while the Seneca and many other tribes, wanting to defend their lands from American encroachment, sided with the British. Inevitably, after the war, many Native Americans who had allied with Britain saw their lands passed to the United States. "In endeavoring to assist you," said a member of the Wea tribe, "it seems we have wrought our own ruin." As so many Native Americans had supported Britain, almost all were now treated as enemies. The Confederation Congress of 1787 might have promised to recognize and protect Native American land rights, but in practice land speculators moved in. American independence was, in the words of historian Gordon S. Wood, "a disaster for the Indians."

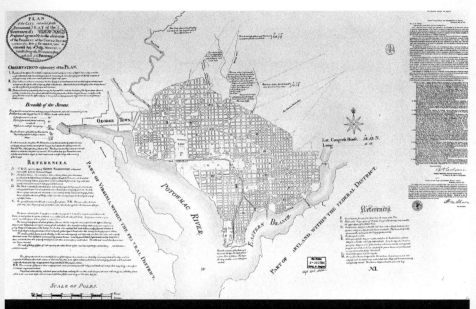

The plan for the capital of Washington on the Potomac River, which, Thomas Jefferson wrote, "offers to pour into our lap the whole commerce of the Western world."

BUILDING A CAPITAL

After independence, Congress moved from town to town at first, but it was soon decided that the new country needed a capital. America's largest city, Philadelphia—with a population of 50,000—was the obvious contender, but no other states were willing to concede to a dominant Pennsylvania. Virginians argued that, as the Potomac River led deep into America's interior, it would make a practical and symbolic location for a new capital.

So it was decided, after some political wrangling, that the capital should be built there as the gateway to America's future in the West.

In 1791, a 10-mile (16-km) square piece of land was carved out of Virginia and Maryland, creating the District of Columbia, where the capital Washington would be built, although for many years it remained a squalid place, marginal to most Americans.

THE AMERICAN FUTURE

With support from France, the 13 colonies had managed to defeat the mother country and had gone on to forge a modern republic. To the east, conflict with Britain and even France was not yet over, while looking westward vast lands lay to be explored and exploited, fought over and conquered.

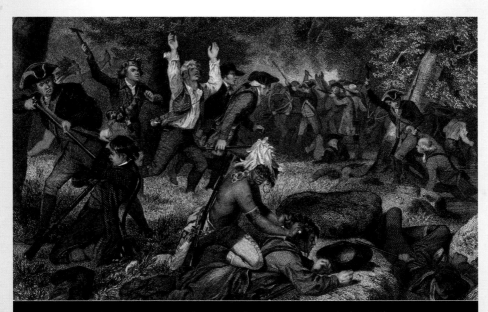

In the Massacre of Wyoming Valley in Pennsylvania in July 1778, Iroquois Native Americans fought alongside the British in defeating the Revolutionaries. The following year, 40 Iroquois villages were destroyed in an effort to crush their morale and their loyalty to the British.

CHAPTER 3

GOING WEST

THROUGH WARS AND LAND PURCHASES, THE UNITED STATES WOULD more than double in size in the first half of the nineteenth century. More space, however, did not mean better treatment for Native Americans, while North and South would become further divided over slavery.

At the end of the War of Independence in 1783, Britain ceded, to America, land west of the Appalachians and north of the Ohio River. Mapping this new territory, Thomas Jefferson, in the Land Ordinance of 1785 and the Northwest Ordinance of 1787, devised a system that said when territories reached populations of 60,000 they could apply to join the Union as a state.

But, were new states to be slave states or free states? This was an

"Old America seems to be breaking up, and moving westward," wrote English traveler Morris Birkbeck in Pennsylvania in 1817. "We are seldom out of sight, as we travel towards the Ohio River, of family groups behind and before us."

issue that would last from the early years of independence until the end of slavery after the Civil War. Despite protests from the South, Congress did prohibit slavery in the new northwest states, although it conceded that slave owners could maintain the right to hunt down fugitive slaves in the new territories.

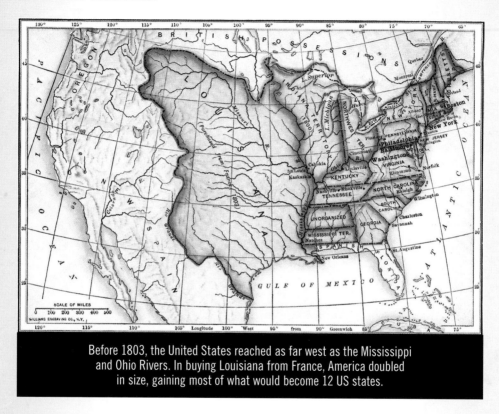

Before 1803, the United States reached as far west as the Mississippi and Ohio Rivers. In buying Louisiana from France, America doubled in size, gaining most of what would become 12 US states.

Beyond the United States, large chunks of North America were still occupied by Britain, France, and Spain. Florida was in Spanish hands, as was the Louisiana Territory, which fanned out in a northwesterly direction from New Orleans and reached right up to the Canadian border. Originally French, the vast area had, in 1763, been ceded to Spain, but in 1800 it passed back to the French. Jefferson wanted New Orleans for America, however, because, as Louisiana's port, it controlled US exports, including tobacco, which passed down the Mississippi. With this in mind, $10 million was offered to France for New Orleans. It soon became clear that France's emperor Napoleon Bonaparte, who was in need of funds for a planned invasion of Britain, was willing to sell not just the city but also the whole of the Louisiana Territory. So, in 1803, Louisiana was sold to the United States for $15 million. How big the territory was, the Americans didn't know exactly, but they understood that they had bought a vast area from the Mississippi to the Rockies. When eventually measured, it turned out to be more than 800,000 square miles (1,300,000 square km). At a stroke, the United States had doubled in size.

THE LEWIS AND CLARK EXPEDITION

Having bought Louisiana, Jefferson sent a team to explore it. The expedition was led by his protégé, Captain Meriwether Lewis, and Lewis's friend, Lieutenant William Clark. They were to travel up the Missouri River, map the new territory and find a passage across to the Pacific coast.

Setting off in 1804 with a party of 32 soldiers, 10 civilians, Clark's slave, and a few Native American guides and interpreters, they navigated their way up the Missouri and crossed the Rocky Mountains at Lemhi Pass (on the present-day Montana–Idaho border). This was the US frontier. French and British fur trappers had been active in the American interior since the eighteenth century, but the Lewis and Clark party were the first US citizens to cross the Continental Divide. From the Rockies, they made their way by canoe down to the Pacific coast, building a fort at the mouth of the Columbia River in Oregon. This was not just to protect themselves, but also for political reasons. It was important to establish an American presence in the area before the British or French did.

Returning to St Louis after two and a half years, both men became governors—Clark of Missouri, Lewis of Louisiana—but within three years Lewis would be dead. Having suffered for a long time from psychotic episodes, one evening he began raging, and before the morning he had shot himself.

The mission, though, had been a great success. Although they had traveled 8,000 miles (12,875 km) into wild and sometimes hostile territory, their journey is remarkable for how well they fared, with their party suffering just one fatality—from a ruptured appendix. They had also had largely friendly encounters with more than 70 native tribes. Only when Blackfeet Native Americans in Montana tried to steal guns did the situation end with two of the Native Americans being shot. Furthermore, although neither Lewis nor Clark was well educated, they had mapped new terrain, written studies of Native American tribes, and had coined almost a thousand terms for

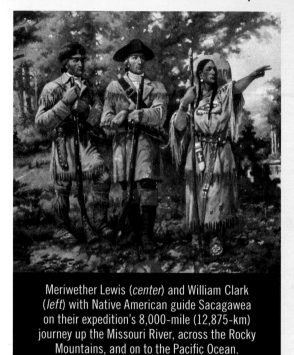

Meriwether Lewis (*center*) and William Clark (*left*) with Native American guide Sacagawea on their expedition's 8,000-mile (12,875-km) journey up the Missouri River, across the Rocky Mountains, and on to the Pacific Ocean.

places, plants, and animals. Without them we might know the "Great Plains" and "grizzly bear" by very different names.

FIRST NATIONS, FOREIGN NATIONS

As America pushed west, Native Americans were repeatedly nudged off the map, or considered "foreign nations" within the new republic. Jefferson saw them as "noble savages" who, at best, would learn to live and farm like white Americans rather than roam as nomadic hunters. Failing that, they would have to remove themselves beyond the Mississippi.

THE LEWIS AND CLARK PARTY WERE THE FIRST US CITIZENS TO CROSS THE CONTINENTAL DIVIDE.

A DUEL WITH THE VICE PRESIDENT

Dueling had been declared illegal in New Jersey, but that didn't stop Jefferson's vice president, Aaron Burr, and the former Secretary of the Treasury, Alexander Hamilton, from drawing pistols in July 1804.

The differences between these two political rivals escalated when Hamilton was quoted in a newspaper as saying that he didn't believe Burr should be "trusted with the reins of government." When Hamilton refused to recant his words and other slurs, Burr made his challenge.

At the duel, both men fired, and Hamilton was mortally wounded. Indicted for murder, Burr fled back to Washington where, beyond the jurisdiction of New Jersey, he was able to see out the final months of his vice presidency in peace. Never brought to trial for the murder, he spent the rest of his life in relative obscurity.

Vice president Aaron Burr kills one of the Founding Fathers, Alexander Hamilton, in a duel in 1804.

Where the Native Americans weren't willing to give up their ancestral lands, violence broke out. Settlers told stories of Native American scalpings and massacres, and, tellingly, in 1789, the US government placed "Indian affairs" under the jurisdiction of the War Department. Then, in 1791, General Arthur St. Clair led an army of 2,000 enlistees into the Ohio Valley to pacify tribes opposed to the expansion. With many of St. Clair's men deserting due to lack of provisions, pay, and training, Native American warriors defeated the Americans, killing around 600 of them,

TO RITUALLY FINISH THE AFFAIR, THE INDIANS STUFFED THE MOUTHS OF DEAD SOLDIERS WITH SOIL.

wounding 300 more, and forcing the remainder to flee. To ritually finish the affair, the Indians stuffed the mouths of dead soldiers with soil. It was the largest defeat in history of a US Army unit by Native Americans.

Although significant, their victory was short-lived. George Washington sent greater numbers of troops against the Ohio Valley Native Americans, and, in August 1794, at Fallen Timbers in northern Ohio, the tribesmen were driven from the field, with hundreds being killed. When the surviving Native Americans fled to Fort Miami (now Maumee, Ohio), the British refused to open the gates as it risked provoking further conflict with the US. Defeated, the Native Americans ceded nearly all of present-day Ohio along with part of Indiana.

In 1809, however, an inspirational chief, Tecumseh, emerged from the Shawnee and pulled together a union of tribes in Ohio country and further south among the Creek. In their thousands, the Native Americans successfully resisted the US until their cause became muddied with international affairs—when the US went to war with Britain.

THE BRITISH ON CAPITOL HILL

How was it that within 30 years of Britain recognizing American independence, the US would declare war on the European power and British redcoats would sack Washington?

At first, the Napoleonic Wars had proved a good commercial opportunity for the US. Jefferson's approach was to let the Europeans have their war and trade with both sides without getting hurt or involved. Both Britain and France, however, saw that as undermining their war efforts and each routinely intercepted American merchant ships they believed to be trading with the other. Once on board the ships, the British not only confiscated goods, but frequently pressganged sailors to serve with them. In all, the Royal Navy kidnapped 3,800 American sailors during this period.

While Britain blocked America's trade with Europe and the West Indies, the US imposed embargoes on Britain, too—although this hurt America more than Britain. In time, France agreed to respect US shipping, but Britain's blockade contin-

Thirty years after winning independence from Britain, the United States declared war on its former European ruler. During the conflict, the British set Washington's public buildings on fire—the only time that the capital has been occupied by a foreign power.

ued. So, in 1812, President James Madison presented the case for war: either the US would fight or accept subordination in international affairs to the British. Congress chose war.

In the two-and-a-half-year conflict there was no major front and most of the land fighting involved American attempts to secure control of Canada. The British, with so many troops tied up in Europe, turned to the Shawnee chief Tecumseh for support. Together, the British and Native American forces occupied Detroit and Fort Dearborn (present-day Chicago), before pulling back to the north side of the Great Lakes. When Tecumseh was killed in battle in 1813, however, his confederacy, lacking his charismatic leadership, fell apart.

Opening a new front the following year, the British attacked Washington, before burning its public buildings, including Capitol Hill and the presidential mansion—which, when painted white after the war, became known as the White House. The last major battle came with the British assault on New Orleans in January 1815. Having launched an attack on the earthworks outside the city, the British had failed to bring any ladders, and their troops were picked off as they clambered over each other's shoulders. Easily victorious, the Americans killed 300 British soldiers while losing just 13 lives on their side. As it happened, the whole assault was in vain: the two countries had already signed a peace treaty a month earlier in Ghent in the United Netherlands, but the news had not yet reached America.

Peace re-established the status quo: the borders remained unchanged and the embargoes were no longer an issue as the Anglo–French wars had ended, while the protection of Native American lands, which the British had called for just months earlier, was not secured.

THE INDIAN REMOVAL ACT

In the southeast, Native Americans had made a great effort to assimilate, accepting Protestant missionaries, establishing schools and even owning slaves. With long traditions of agriculture and settlement rather than nomadic life, they were better suited than other tribes to follow European models. After three centuries of European presence, blood was now often mixed. John Ross,

Despite protestations from northern states, the Indian Removal Act was passed in 1830, paving the way for the forced expulsion of tens of thousands of Native Americans from their homelands in America's southeast.

chief of the Cherokee, for instance, was the son of a Scottish trader and a part Native American mother. A successful cotton producer and slave owner, he encouraged assimilation in politics. Among their own people, the Cherokee adopted a two-house legislature and a judicial system. But Ross also argued for Cherokee rights, to the extent that in 1827 the Cherokee, largely located in Georgia, declared their independence from the US.

Not only was this anathema to the white people of Georgia, the following year gold was discovered on Cherokee land, and Georgia's state legislature passed a law affirming that all the Cherokee came under its jurisdiction. The Cherokee responded that their sovereignty was negotiated with the federal government, not state law.

Making it a federal matter did not help the Cherokee—President Andrew Jackson was fully in favor of Native American removal. In his first State of the Union message in December 1829, Jackson asked: "What good man would prefer a country covered with forest and ranged by a few thousand savages to our extensive republic, studded with cities, towns and prospective farms?" He requested that Congress set aside "an ample district west of the Mississippi" for Native American tribes to live in under their own governments with minimal control from Washington. If they were to remain, the Native Americans would have to be subject to state laws.

To the Protestant North, where there were few Native Americans left, the suggestion of removing the Native Americans westwards, and failing to convert them to Christianity, was received with horror. Was that the behavior of a country founded on "life, liberty and the pursuit of happiness"? As Senator Theodore Frelinghuysen of New Jersey pointed out: "We successfully and triumphantly contended for the very rights and privileges that our Indian neighbors now implore us to protect." Nevertheless, the Indian Removal Act was passed in 1830.

Of the "Five Civilized Tribes" in the Southeast, the Chickasaw Nation, Choctaw, and Creek were the first to sign up for removal and swap their territory for land further west. The Seminole in Florida, however, fought back, claiming that the treaty had been forced upon them. It would take six years and 1,500 American dead before they were crushed, with many Native Americans dead or forcibly removed, leaving just pockets of tribespeople who had been joined by runaway slaves.

Meanwhile the Cherokee, led by John Ross, fought on, but through the courts rather than on the battlefield. In 1831, Ross took his suit, that it was a federal not a state matter, to the Supreme Court. Two justices agreed with him; the other five did

THE AMERICANS KILLED 300 BRITISH SOLDIERS WHILE LOSING JUST 13 LIVES ON THEIR SIDE.

John Ross, chief of the Cherokee, was the son of a Scottish trader and a part Native American mother. A successful cotton producer, he attempted to resist the removal of his tribe westward, not by waging war, but through the US courts.

not. With legal channels exhausted, the Cherokee were finally pushed out of their homes at gunpoint. Herded into stockades, hundreds died of malnutrition and dysentery. The survivors, about 13,000, were marched west of the Mississippi, with a quarter dying on the way. The new land in the west was guaranteed by the US government—but the same had been said about the land the Native Americans had just lost.

In the 1820s, about 125,000 Indians lived east of the Mississippi. Twenty years later there were only 30,000, mostly on reservations around the Great Lakes. Freed up, the land in the southeast could now be exploited for an industry that was surging ahead: cotton production.

SLAVES

What kind of future did this new, optimistic republic promise its slaves? Although Pennsylvania became the first state to abolish slavery in 1780, that did not spell immediate liberty. Slaves were economic assets to be exploited,

HERDED INTO STOCKADES, HUNDREDS DIED OF MALNUTRITION AND DYSENTERY.

so the new law meant that no slave born before March 1 of that year in the state was freed, and that any slave born after March 1 would not be freed until the age of 28. That way, there would not be any free slaves in Pennsylvania until 1808 at the earliest.

Still, by 1804, all the Northern states, where there were about 30,000 slaves, had introduced similar laws that would gradually abolish slavery. In 1808, Congress voted to end US participation in the African slave trade within two years. Despite more than 150,000 slaves being shipped to the US between 1801 and 1810—the highest figure for any decade in American history—it must have seemed that, with the new legislation, slavery was about to die out in the US.

In fact, the opposite was true. The ending of America's involvement in the Atlantic trade only increased the value in the domestic slave market. Owners now bred slaves for sale, and, as the Southern states introduced slavery into new states, demand increased. Across the Americas as a whole, the US had imported the smallest proportion of African slaves, but by the time of the Civil War in 1861 it would be home to four million, the largest slave population in both North and South America.

The demand for slaves was driven by cotton production. With mechanical innovations, short-staple cotton could now be produced 50 times more quickly than in the eighteenth century—if there were the hands to pick it. Using slave labor, it could be a profitable product for the world market, and production expanded right across the South.

Jefferson certainly appreciated the injustice of slavery, but he also understood the economy of the South and depended on 200 slaves to work his own Virginia plantation. Although he believed that Native Americans could be "civilized" to become Americans, he felt that blacks and whites were bound by their slave–master relationship, and that the best future for black people would be to establish their own nations in Africa, even though many of them had never been there.

So, at the same time that slaves in the North were beginning to experience their freedom, slavery in the South was being strengthened. After months of political debate as to whether new states would be slave states or free, in 1820 Congress drew an east–west line through the country, stating that all new states north of 36 degrees 30 minutes, would be barred to slavery. Known as the Missouri Compromise, this may have temporarily settled the matter, but it effectively partitioned the country, reinforcing the divisions between North and South. Jefferson prophetically referred to it as "a fire bell in the night."

DENMARK VESEY AND NAT TURNER

If lottery winners are usually remembered for their frivolous spending, slave Denmark Vesey was the exception: in 1800, he won $1,500 on a lottery and with it bought his freedom. A carpenter by trade, Vesey went on to lead a breakaway black Methodist church in Charleston, South Carolina. His fiery rhetoric called for slaves to fight for their freedom, but in 1822 Vesey was convicted of plotting a slave revolt. What was really being

Captured after his slave rebellion was crushed, Nat Turner was tried and executed.

planned is unclear and was probably exaggerated by white leaders, but Vesey and 30 others were hanged.

Nine years later, slave Nat Turner led a rebellion of more than 70 slaves and free blacks in Virginia. As they moved from plantation to plantation freeing slaves, more than 55 white men, women, and children were killed. The retaliation, however, was even bloodier. Although the rebellion was crushed within two days, more than 200 black people, many uninvolved in the rebellion, were subsequently killed by a white mob. Convicted, Turner was hanged, beheaded, and quartered. Fifteen other slaves and one free black man were also hanged, while 12 slaves were sold out of state.

After the successful anti-slavery revolution in Haiti (1791–1804), Nat Turner's rising had confirmed Southern fears of a slave insurrection and states now passed laws restricting slaves, like Vesey, from gaining their freedom.

TEXAS AND MEXICO

By 1821, the US was no longer the only United States in North America. The United States of Mexico had just gained its independence from colonial Spain, and, reaching across the southwest of North America and far up the Pacific Coast, it was roughly the same size as the US. But it was Catholic and didn't permit slavery, which proved to be a problem for the American settlers pushing into its states of Texas and California. With slaves making up 20 percent of the US population, the 40,000 settlers in Texas had no intention of changing their ways—so much so that in 1835 they declared Texas an independent state.

It was a bold move, but Mexico wasn't going to let Texas go. Troops were sent in, skirmishes followed, and, after a 13-day siege, on March 6,

A statue of Denmark Vesey, erected in Charleston, South Carolina, in 2014.

1836, numerically superior Mexican forces stormed the Alamo fort near San Antonio. In the battle, 600 Mexicans died, and all the Texan and American defenders, more than 180 of them, were killed. The following month, a Texan-American force led by Sam Houston—with the famous rallying cry of "Remember the Alamo!"—surprised the Mexican Army, defeating the enemy in 20 minutes at the Battle of San Jacinto.

Although Mexico now conceded independence to the new Republic of Texas, this didn't mean that the territory would automatically become part of the US. That would have upset the delicate balance struck between the number of slave states and free states, which had been maintained by only allowing them to enter in pairs: one slave state with one free state. Therefore, Texas's destiny remained uncertain for almost a decade.

An auction house in Atlanta, Georgia, photographed by George N. Barnard during the Union occupation of the city during the Civil War. The man reading is an African American soldier from the Union Army.

PROMISED LAND

During this period, America was changing—it was building, and very quickly. In 1825, its first man-made waterway, the 363-mile (584-km) Erie Canal, connecting the Hudson River with Lake Erie, was opened; within 15 years, America would have more than 3,300 miles (5311 km) of canals. In the same period, it built just as many miles of railway, almost double that of Europe. As well as transport, the telegraph, which was pioneered in the US in the 1830s, offered a rapid form of long-distance communication.

The result was that the idea of a nation reaching from the Atlantic to the Pacific became both conceivable and within reach. Internationally, the US was a pioneer, too, dominating the whaling industry and establishing links with China as early as 1784, where they undercut the British East India Company.

Former congressman and frontiersman Davy Crockett wields his rifle like a club as the Texan defenders are overrun by Mexican soldiers at the Alamo.

While the population of the US nearly doubled over these years, Mexico remained largely agrarian, its fragile union of states near to collapse, and its population only increasing slightly to seven million.

With expansionist fervor at full rein, in 1844 the emerging American Democrat Party began campaigning for the "re-annexation of Texas"—although, in truth, Texas had never been properly annexed in the first place. Legislation was pushed through Congress, and, in 1845, Texas became a state, with US troops asserting a claim of a border with Mexico along the Rio Grande, much further south than the existing frontier. At the same time, an envoy was sent to Mexico City offering up to $40 million for New Mexico and California.

The envoy's offers were flatly rejected. But, when Mexican troops crossed the Rio Grande and left 16 US soldiers dead or wounded, the new

Democrat president, James K. Polk, used the pretext to call for military action, claiming that Mexico had "invaded our territory and shed American blood on American soil."

Mexican resistance in Texas proved stronger than anticipated, however, and the war dragged on for two years (1846–48). Finally, the US invaded Mexico, blockaded its ports and occupied Mexico City, forcing the Mexicans to the negotiating table. The ensuing Treaty of Guadalupe Hidalgo, signed in February 1848, gave the US all of the provinces of New Mexico and California in exchange for $15 million—the same price that they had paid for

FINALLY, THE US INVADED MEXICO, BLOCKADED ITS PORTS AND OCCUPIED MEXICO CITY.

the Louisiana Territory almost 50 years earlier, but for even more land. Mexico lost half of its landmass, while the land the US gained—what would become the states of Arizona, New Mexico, Nevada, Utah and California—makes up roughly a quarter of the nation today.

The California Gold Rush of 1849 was followed by later mineral discoveries across the West—silver in Nevada, gold in Colorado, copper in Montana, and zinc in Idaho. Here, prospectors wash and pan for gold in the Dakota Territory in 1889.

THE DONNER PARTY

Going west full of the pioneering spirit of "manifest destiny"—the mid-century concept that the land was America's God-given right to inhabit—wasn't, understandably, sufficient to ensure a safe arrival. Many people perished on the journey, either from hostile encounters with Native Americans, drowning at river crossings, thirst, or starvation. Some of the worst hardships were suffered by the Donner Party. In May 1846, a loose train of pioneering families, led by George Donner and numbering 90 adults and children, left Independence, Missouri, for California, a journey of more than 1400 miles (2253 km). Rather than taking the established Oregon Trail, they followed a new route plotted by adventurer and author Lansford W. Hastings, which crossed Utah's Wasatch Mountains and the Great Salt Lake Desert. Instead of saving time, as Hastings had boasted, this added 150 miles (240 km) to their journey, meaning that it was already November when they reached the Sierra Nevada mountain range.

With snow falling unusually early, the families soon found themselves snowbound. Seeking help, a party of the 17 strongest members set out for Sutter's Fort near Sacramento, California, more than 100 miles (160km) away. With only six days of provisions—the most the party could afford to spare—they were soon starving. When members began to die, the others resorted to cannibalism, labeling the human meat so that no one would eat their own kin. After six weeks crossing the mountains, just seven survivors reached the fort and found help.

Those who had remained at the mountain camps also cannibalized their dead before the rescue party reached them in the spring. In all, 47 of the original 90 members of the Donner Party survived the crossing.

California could be bountiful, but reaching it was largely a journey into the unknown, trusting, in this case, Hastings's unfounded claims of a shortcut. J. Quinn Thornton, who had travelled part of the route with the Donner Party, later dubbed Hastings the "Baron Munchausen of travellers."

Stranded crossing the Sierra Nevada mountains in the winter of 1846, some members of the Donner Party began to die of starvation. Others were later forced to cannibalize the dead to survive.

The shape of modern America was now taking form. Two years earlier, the US had come to an agreement with Britain over the northern border, dividing the Northwest along the 49th Parallel. This pushed the British out of Oregon County, but gave both countries access to the Juan de Fuca Strait, allowing Britain to build an ice-free port at Vancouver.

THE GOLD RUSH

The drive of people westwards surged with the discovery of gold in California in 1848. Two years earlier, there had been about 10,000 people in California; by 1849, there were 80,000, and, by 1860, there were 380,000 non-Indian people. But the newcomers weren't all from the US: within two years, 25,000 Chinese had arrived, along with Latin Americans, Australians, and Europeans.

With California not yet a state, it was a near-lawless place allowing prospectors to take what land they wanted for free, rather than having to buy land off the government as they did elsewhere. That said, few of the prospectors got really rich; canny merchants supplying the miners did better. Levi Strauss, for instance, had gone west with the intention of selling canvas for tents before realizing that the biggest demand lay in hard-wearing denim trousers. Laundries, boarding houses, and brothels sprang up to cater for the new population. Boomtowns quickly developed, but could just as quickly become ghost towns once the gold ore was exhausted or easier pickings were found elsewhere. Ships in the port of San Francisco were even abandoned by their crews, who, on arrival, joined the rush. With the unmanned boats clogging up the harbor, many were broken up and the wood used for new housing in the rapidly expanding city.

Native Americans once again suffered as the prospectors pushed them off their land or allowed the silt from mines to poison their crops. This led to violent conflicts. One of the bloodiest was the 1852 Bridge Gulch Massacre in California, when more than 150 Wintu were killed by about

70 Americans led by the sheriff of Trinity County in a revenge attack after the Wintu had killed a US colonel. It later emerged that the Wintu whom the Americans butchered were not responsible for the colonel's death.

THE COMPROMISE OF 1850

The growth in population in California led by the Gold Rush once again unsettled the balance between North and South. As the population in the more urbanized North and in the West was increasing at a far greater rate than in the South, free states would have more seats in the House of Representatives—seats being based on each state's population. If this trend were to continue, argued Senator John C. Calhoun of South Carolina in 1850, a Congress dominated by free states would force the South to choose "between abolition and secession." He was right.

Despite protestations from abolitionists, when California entered the Union as a free state, a concession was made to slave states: henceforth, runaway slaves caught in free states had to be returned to their Southern owners.

To avert abolition or secession—for the time being, at least—when California entered the Union as a free state in 1850, a concession was made to the South in the form of the Fugitive Slave Law. Citizens were forbidden from helping fugitive slaves, and Northern states would be required to assist the South in returning fleeing slaves to their masters.

LAND OF THE FREE

By 1850, the US reached east–west from the Atlantic to the Pacific, its borders were largely settled, its cities growing, its industries thriving. However, the division between North and South, between slave states and free states, had only become more entrenched as the first half of the nineteenth century progressed. Soon it would pitch the nation into civil war.

GLOSSARY

American Civil War The war in the United States of America between 11 newly seceded southern states (the South), called the Confederate States of America, and the states of the Union (the North) when tensions between free states and slave states debated the power of the national government to prohibit slavery.

annex To append or add as an extra or subordinate part, especially to a document. Countries can annex territory, such as states, in certain situations.

Common Sense A pamphlet written by Thomas Paine in 1775--76 about the prospect of colonial independence from Great Britain.

emigration The act of leaving one's place of residence, or country, to live elsewhere.

First Americans The ancient people believed to be the first inhabitants of the American continent, commonly believed to have migrated from Northeast Asia.

gold rush When a population moves in response to newly discovered goldfields and mining prospects. This is the nickname given to the western migration of peoples in the United States to California in 1848 in response to the gold discovered.

Missouri Compromise An attempt by Congress to draw an east-west line through the country, stating that all new states north of 36 degrees, 30 minutes, would be barred to slavery, as an attempt to balance the number of slave states and free states admitted.

Redcoats A term for soldiers in the armies of Great Britain, referring to their commonly red-colored coats.

Revolutionary War Also known as a part of the American Revolution, the war between the American colonies and Great Britain that resulted in American independence.

slavery An act or system in which people are owned as property and afforded minimal or no rights.

FOR MORE INFORMATION

American Historical Association
400 A Street SE
Washington, DC 20003
(202) 544-2422
Website: *https://www.historians.org/*
This organization unites and encourages historians and any aspiring persons interested in any field related to history, through fund-raisers, educational programs, and more.

California Historical Society
678 Mission Street
San Francisco, CA, 94105
(415) 357-1848
Website: *https://www.californiahistoricalsociety.org/*
California's Historical Society maintains museums, educational outreach, and general support in the study of California's historical significance in the United States.

Museum of the American Revolution
101 South Third Street
Philadelphia, PA 19106
(215) 253-6731
Website: *https://www.amrevmuseum.org/*
The museum tells an in-depth story of the American Revolution in period-focused exhibits, films, artifacts, and interactive programs.

National Congress of American Indians (NCAI)
1516 P Street NW
Washington, DC 20005
(202) 466-7767
Website: *http://www.ncai.org/*
Founded in 1944, the NCAI is the largest and oldest organization existing to promote relations between tribes for the purposes of protecting and promoting education, civil rights, history, and other Native American initiatives.

New York Historical Society Museum and Library
170 Central Park West at Richard Gilder Way (77th Street)
New York, NY 10024
(212) 873-3400
Website: *http://www.nyhistory.org/*
The museum and library contains two million manuscripts, 500,000 photographs, 400,000 prints, and other research and graphic histories of New York.

Smithsonian National Museum of African American History and Culture
15th St. and Constitution Avenue NW
Washington, DC 20230
(202) 633-1000
Website: *https://nmaahc.si.edu/*
Though this addition to the Smithsonian only opened in 2016, it has received more than one million visitors and hosts exhibits, artifacts, and speakers related to the history of African American culture.

FURTHER READING

Allmendinger Jr., David F. *Nat Turner and the Rising in Southampton County.* Baltimore, MD: John Hopkins University Press, 2014.

Bowes, John P. *Land Too Good for Indians: Northern Indian Removal.* (New Directions in Native American Studies). Norman, OK: University of Oklahoma Press, 2016.

Brown, Richard D. *Self-Evident Truths: Contesting Equal Rights from the Revolution to the Civil War.* New Haven, CT: Yale University Press, 2017.

Davis, Kenneth C. *In the Shadow of Liberty: The Hidden History of Slavery, Four Presidents, and Five Black Lives.* Harrisonburg, VA: Henry Holt and Company, 2016.

Dunbar-Ortiz, Roxanne. *An Indigenous Peoples' History of the United States* (ReVisioning American History). Boston, MA: Beacon Press, 2014.

Hixson, W. *American Settler Colonialism: A History.* New York, NY: Palgrave MacMillan, 2013.

Kurutz, Gary F. *Gold Rush Stories: 49 Tales of Seekers, Scoundrels, Loss, and Luck.* East Peoria, IL: Heyday, 2017.

Randall, Willard Sterne. *Unshackling America: How the War of 1812 Truly Ended the American Revolution.* New York, NY: St. Martin's Press, 2017.

Saldaña-Portillo, María Josefina. *Indian Given: Racial Geographies across Mexico and the United States* (Latin America Otherwise). Durham, NC: Duke University Press, 2016.

Walters, Kerry. *American Slave Revolts and Conspiracies: A Reference Guide.* Santa Barbara, CA: ABC-CLIO, 2015.

INDEX